AF723775

MYTHIC TEXTURE

MYTHIC TEXTURE BY AKEM

PUBLISHED BY

MYTHIC TEXTURE MEDIA
WWW.MYTHICTEXTURE.COM

PERMISSIONS: INFO@MYTHICTEXTURE.COM

ILLUSTRATOR/WRITER: AKEM
BOOK DESIGNER: ANDREA MILLER
COPY EDITOR: REBECCA COATES

SOFTCOVER ISBN: 9781738840632

WE ACKNOWLEDGE THE SUPPORT OF THE CANADA COUNCIL FOR THE ARTS

Canada Council for the Arts | Conseil des arts du Canada

ACKNOWLEDGMENTS

EJIWA EBENEBE
ODERA IGBOKWE
PHILLIP BOUTTE JR.
ERIC WILKERSON
JAZ PAPADOPOULOS

SPACEFARERS

A SPARK in the void
the Painter
of the Night
appears

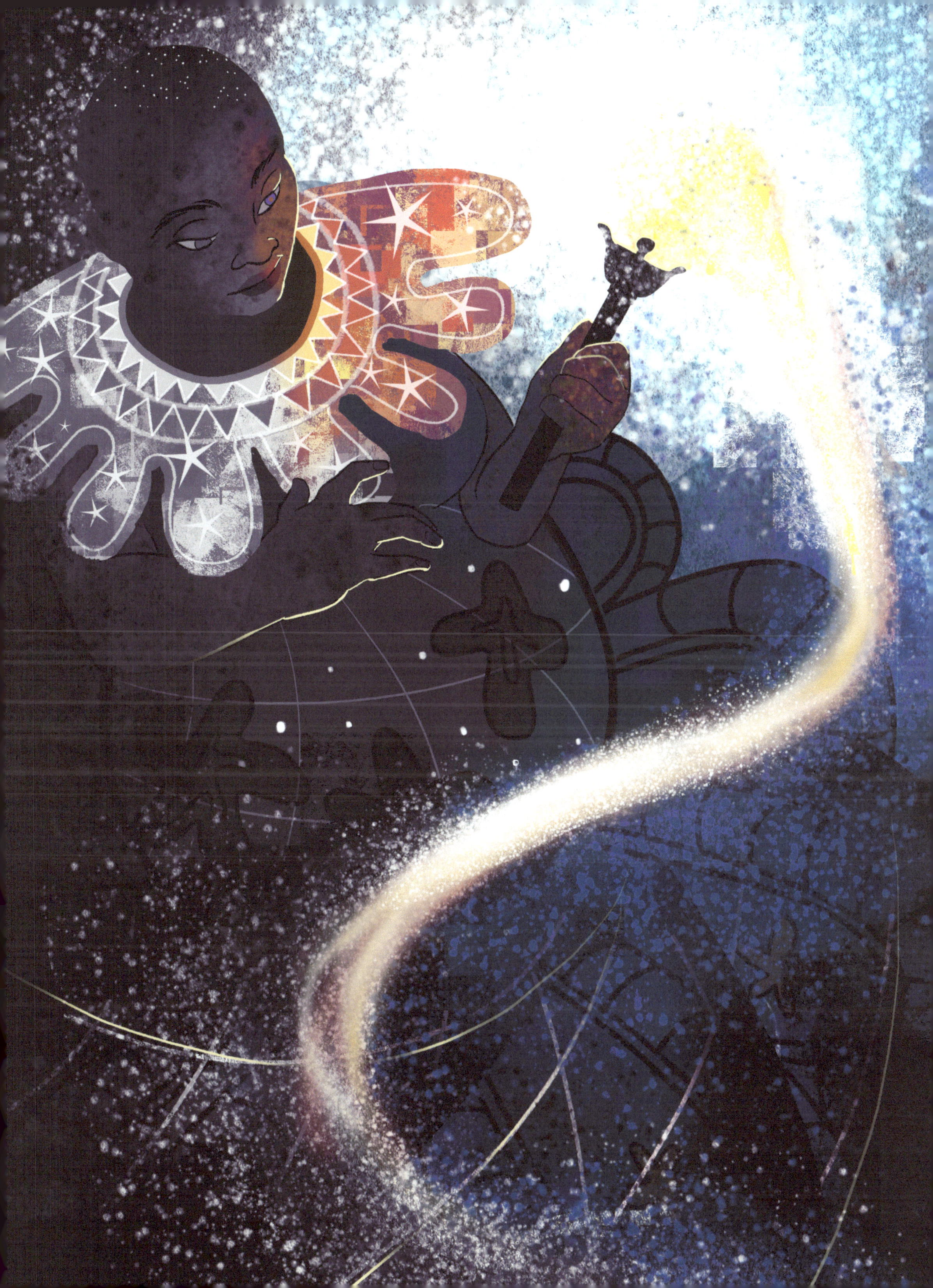

IGNITING

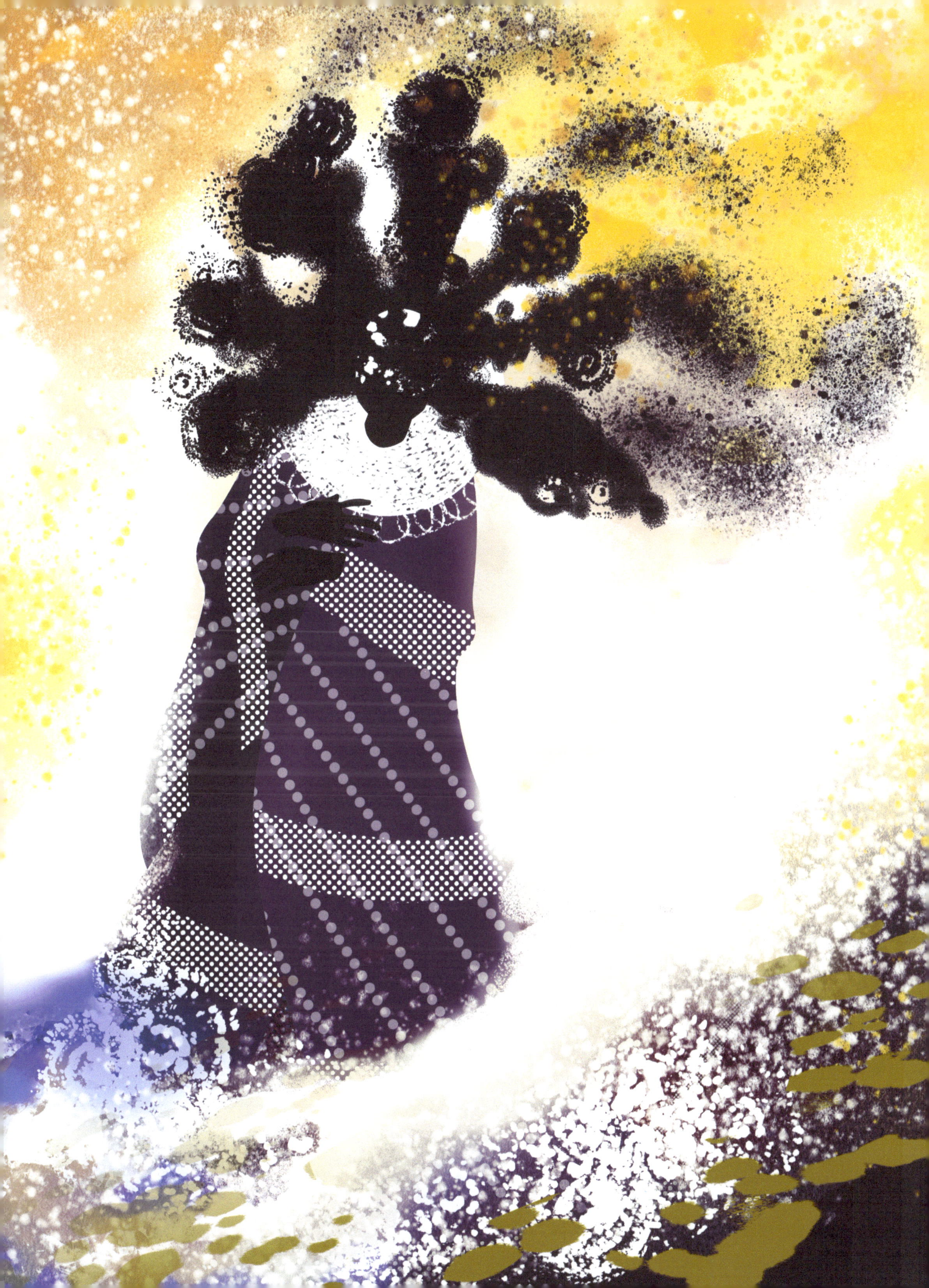

a DREAM

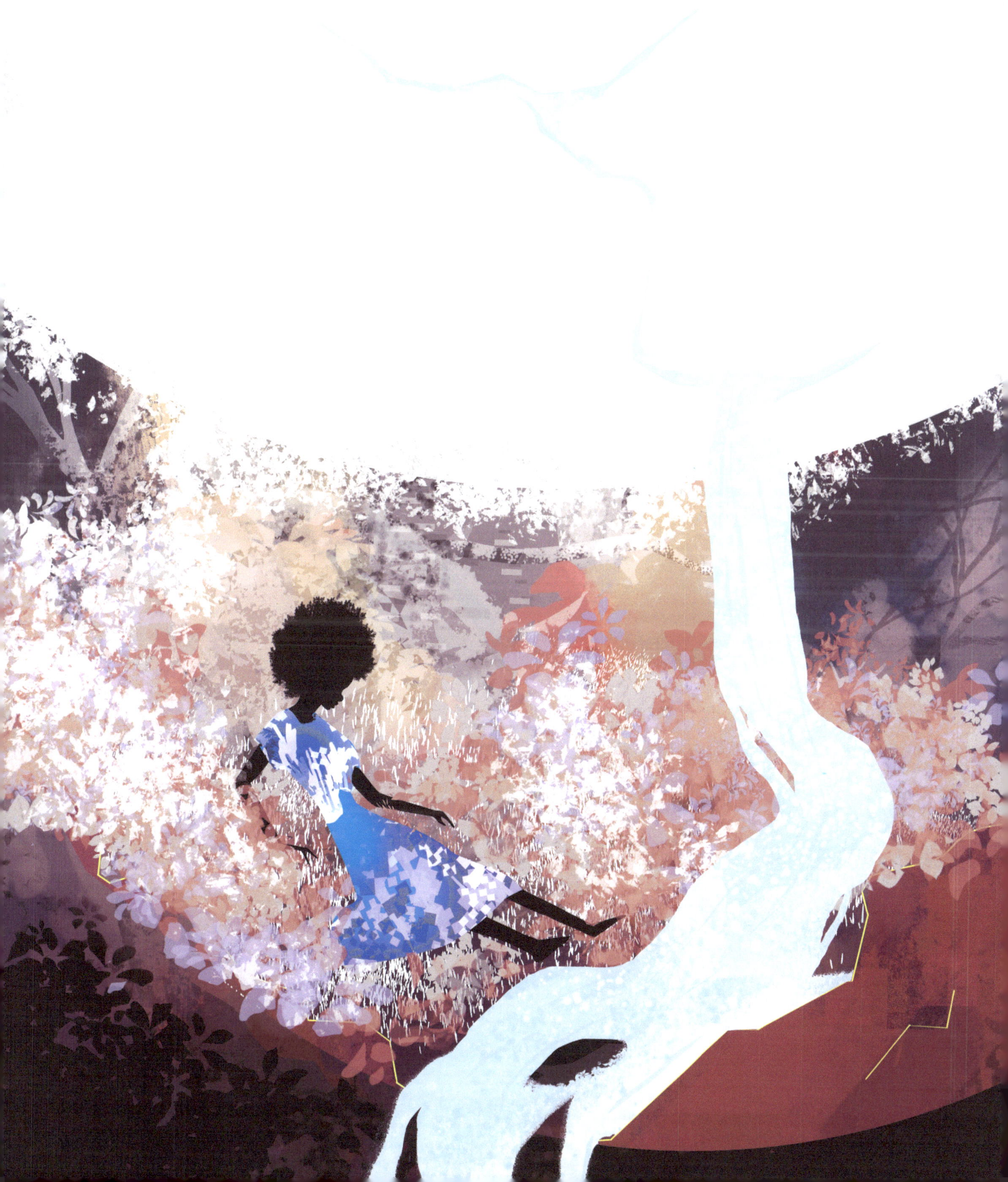

of a distant earth

being SEEDED with life

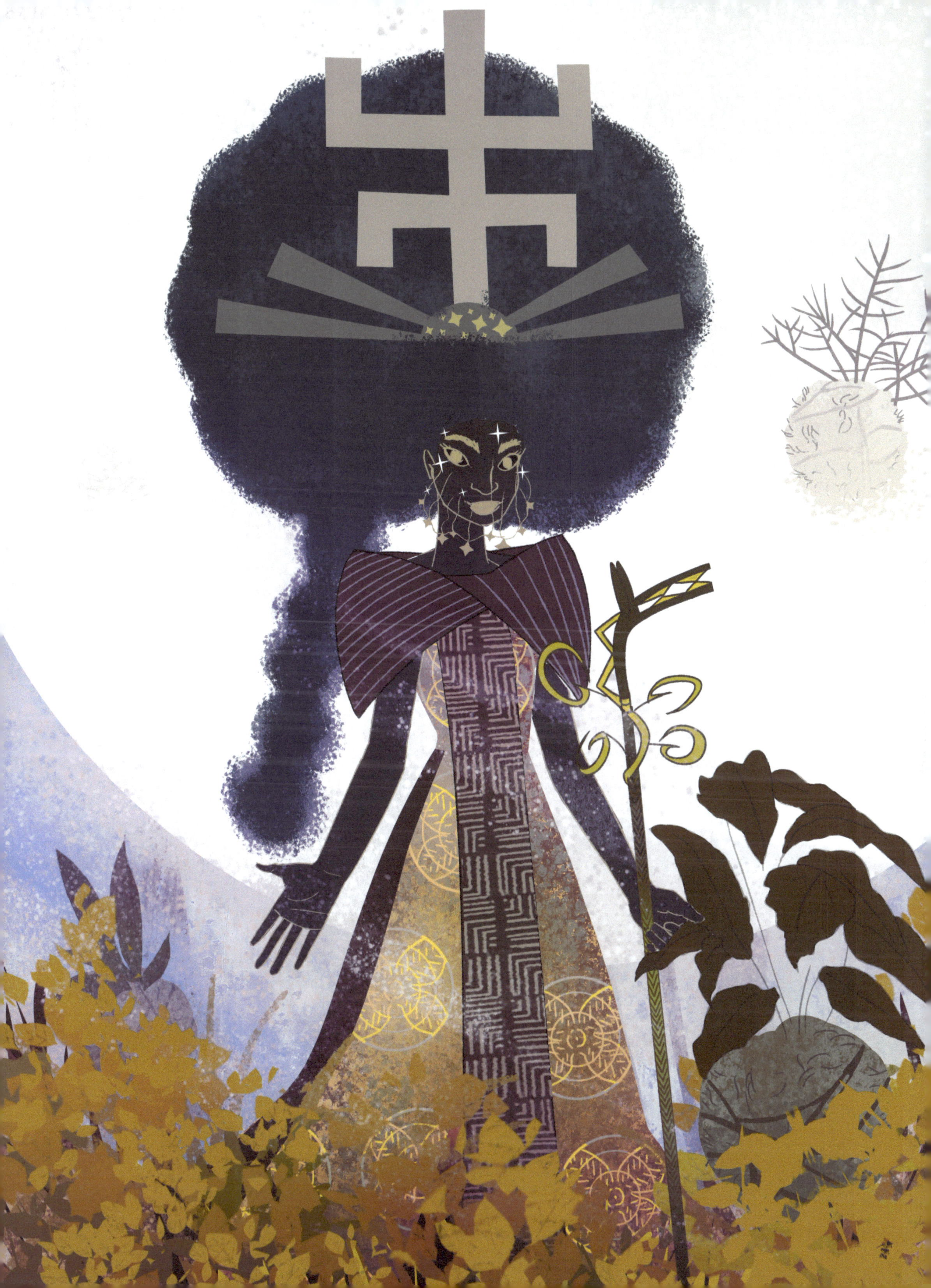

and Stardust being

GATHERED

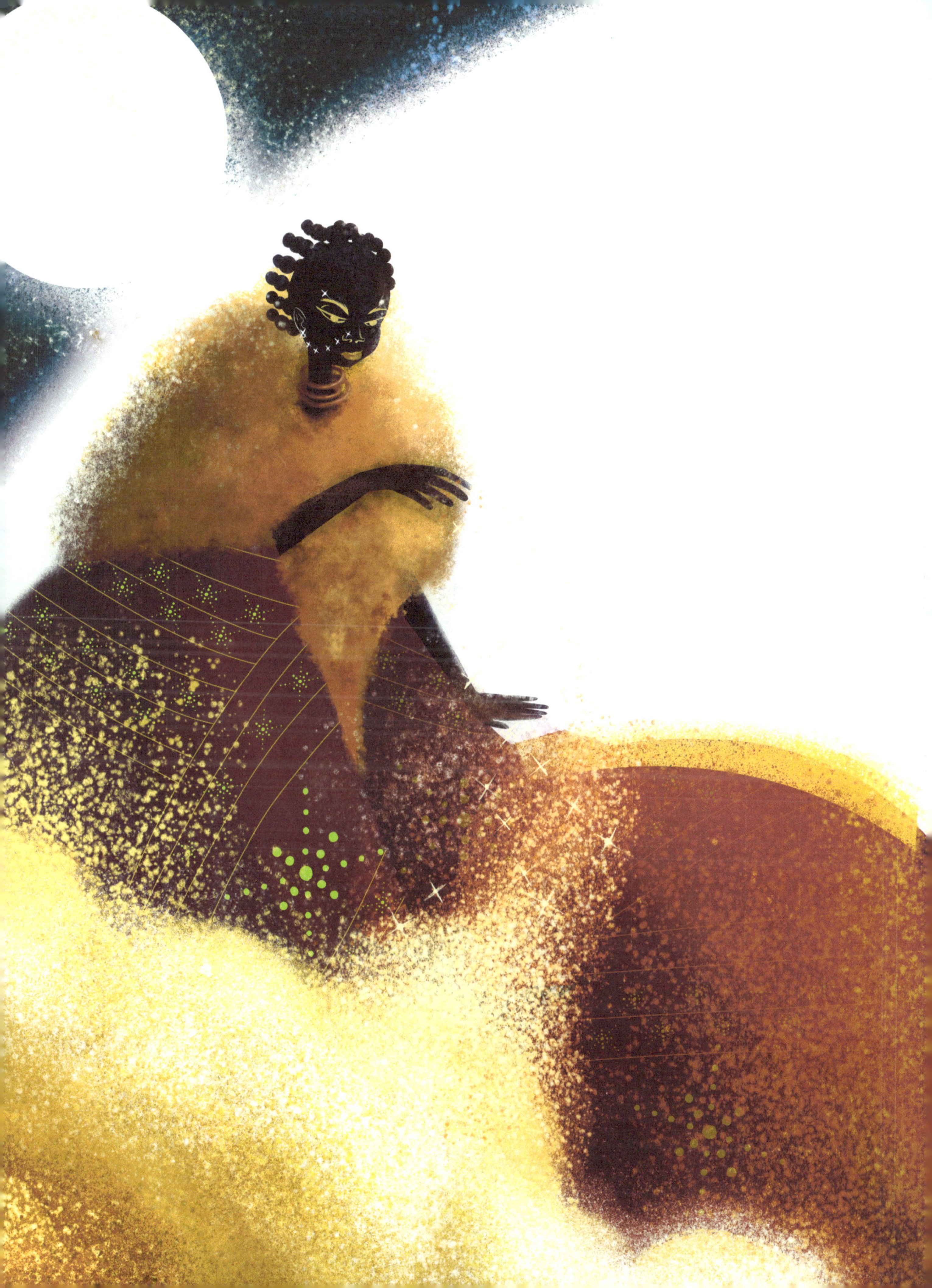

for the Starmaker's

DESIGNS.

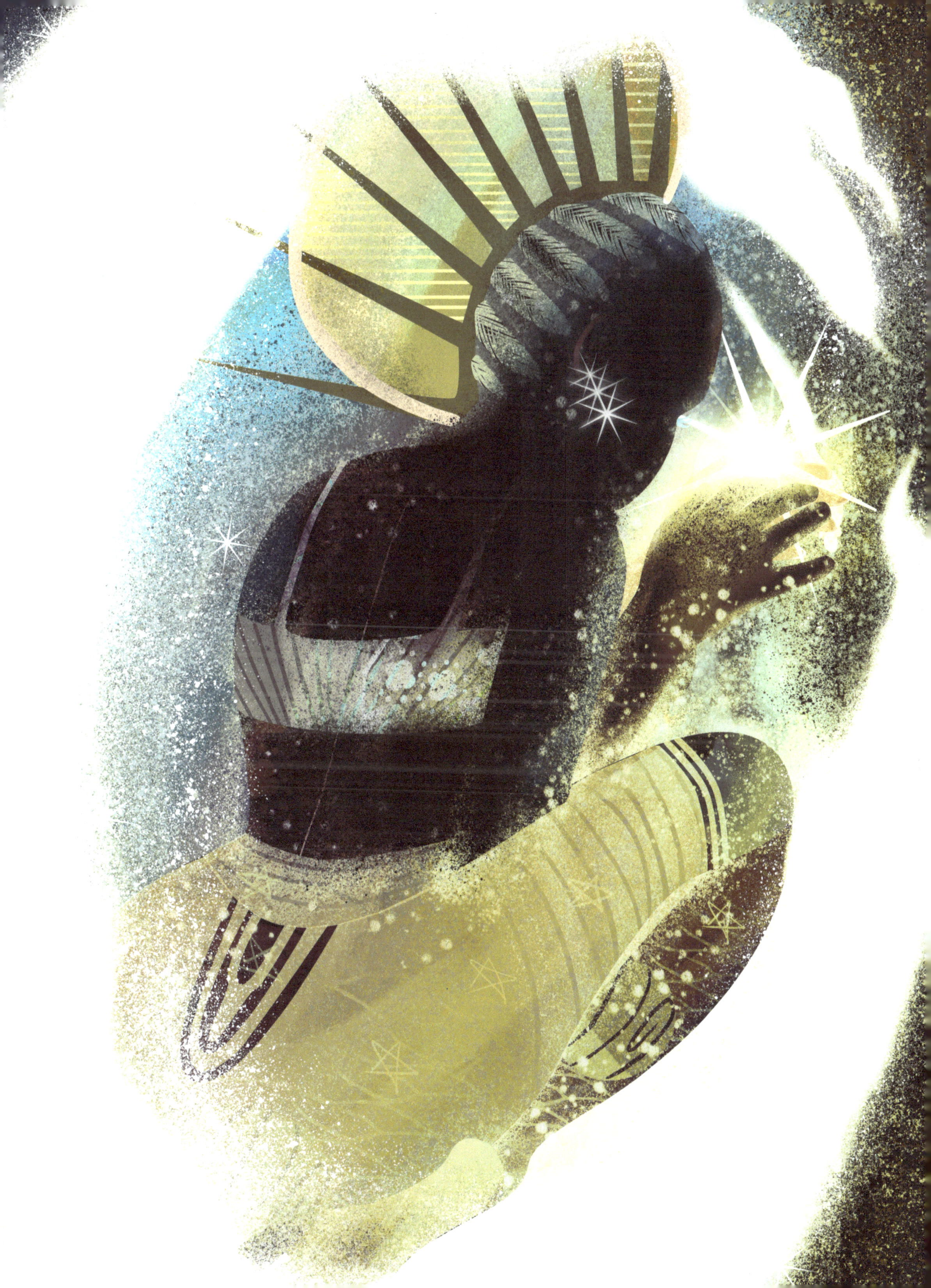

the Wanderer OBSERVES

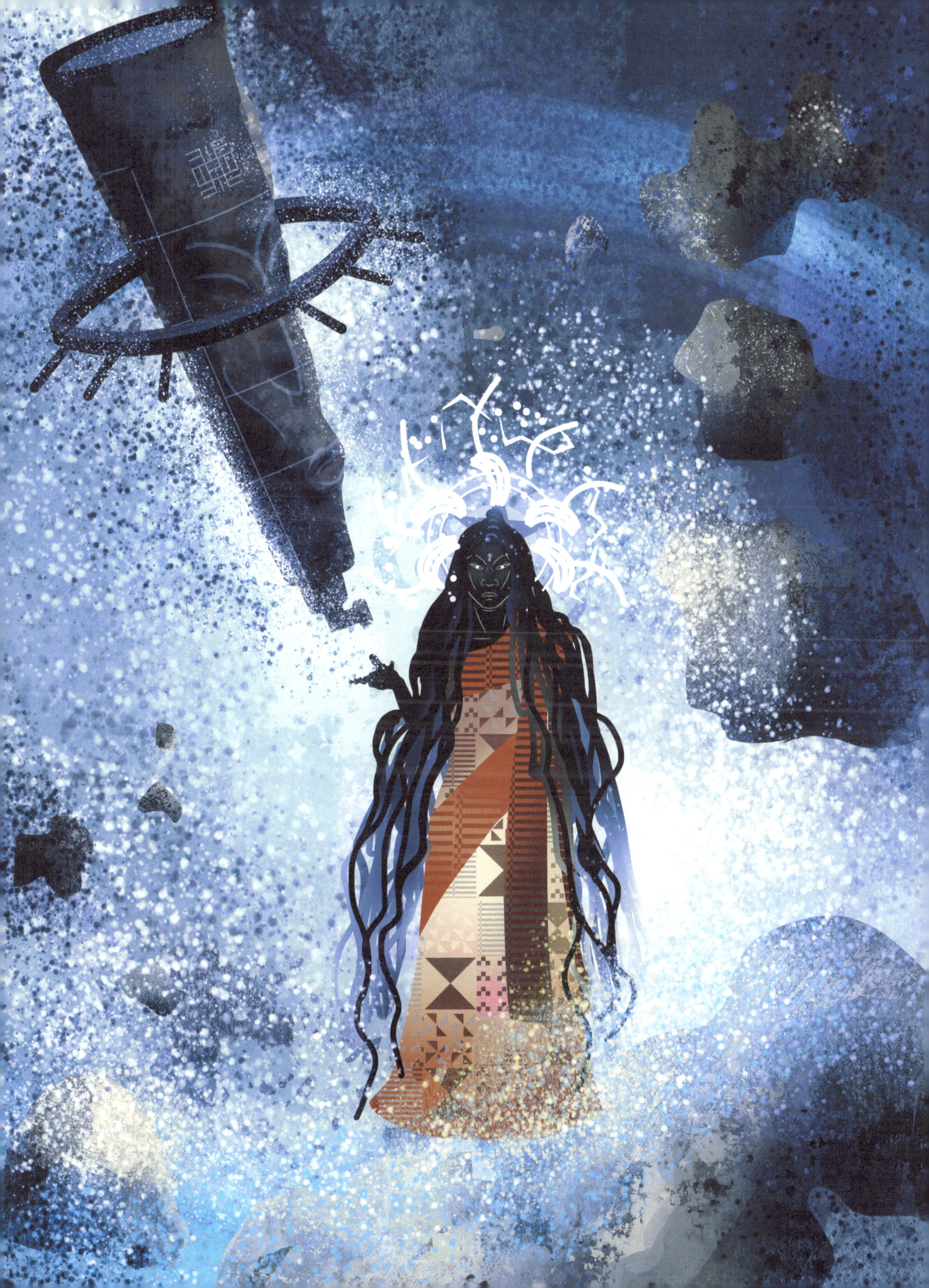

Starwind BLOWING
the stars
and planets
into place,

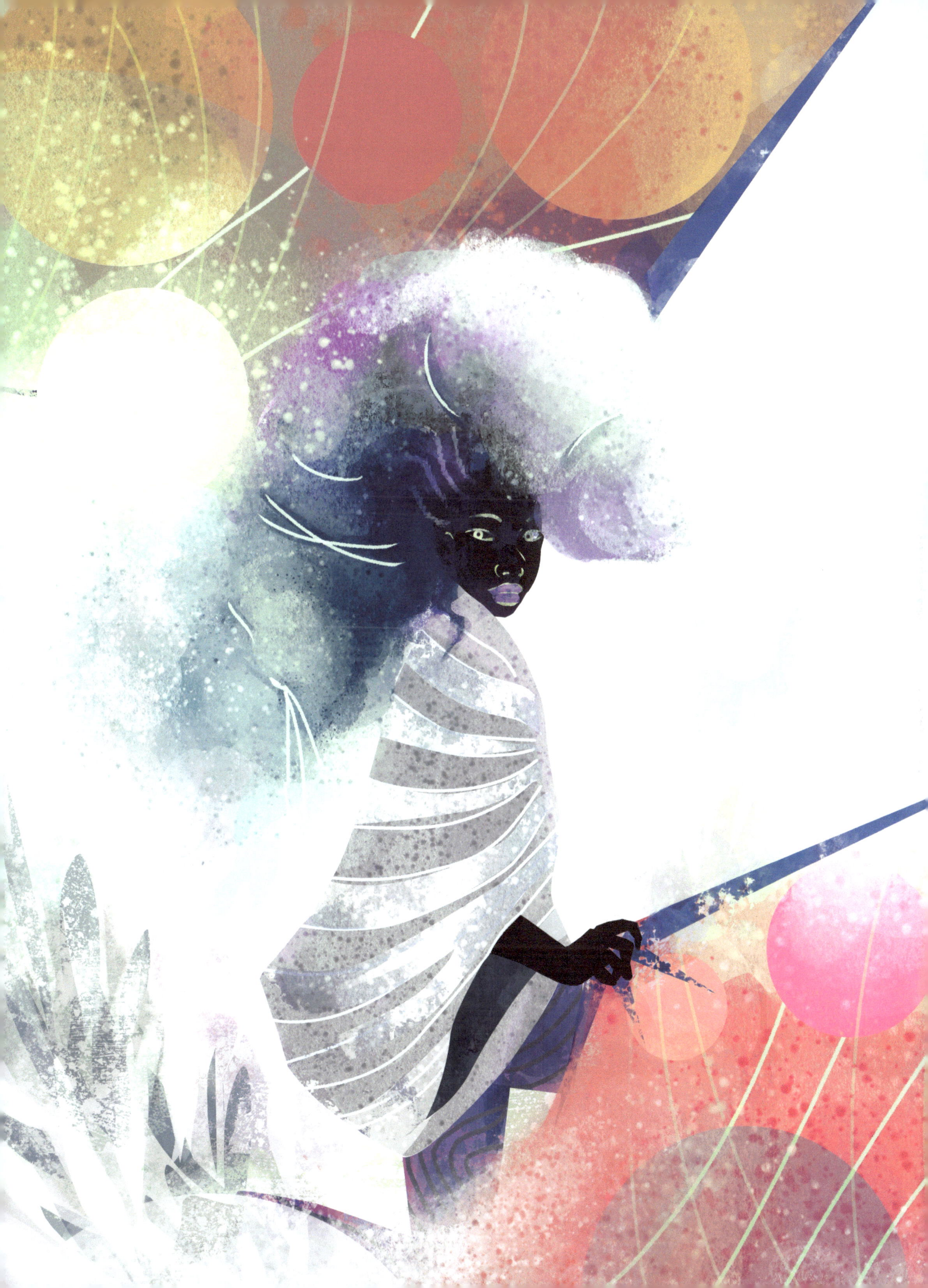

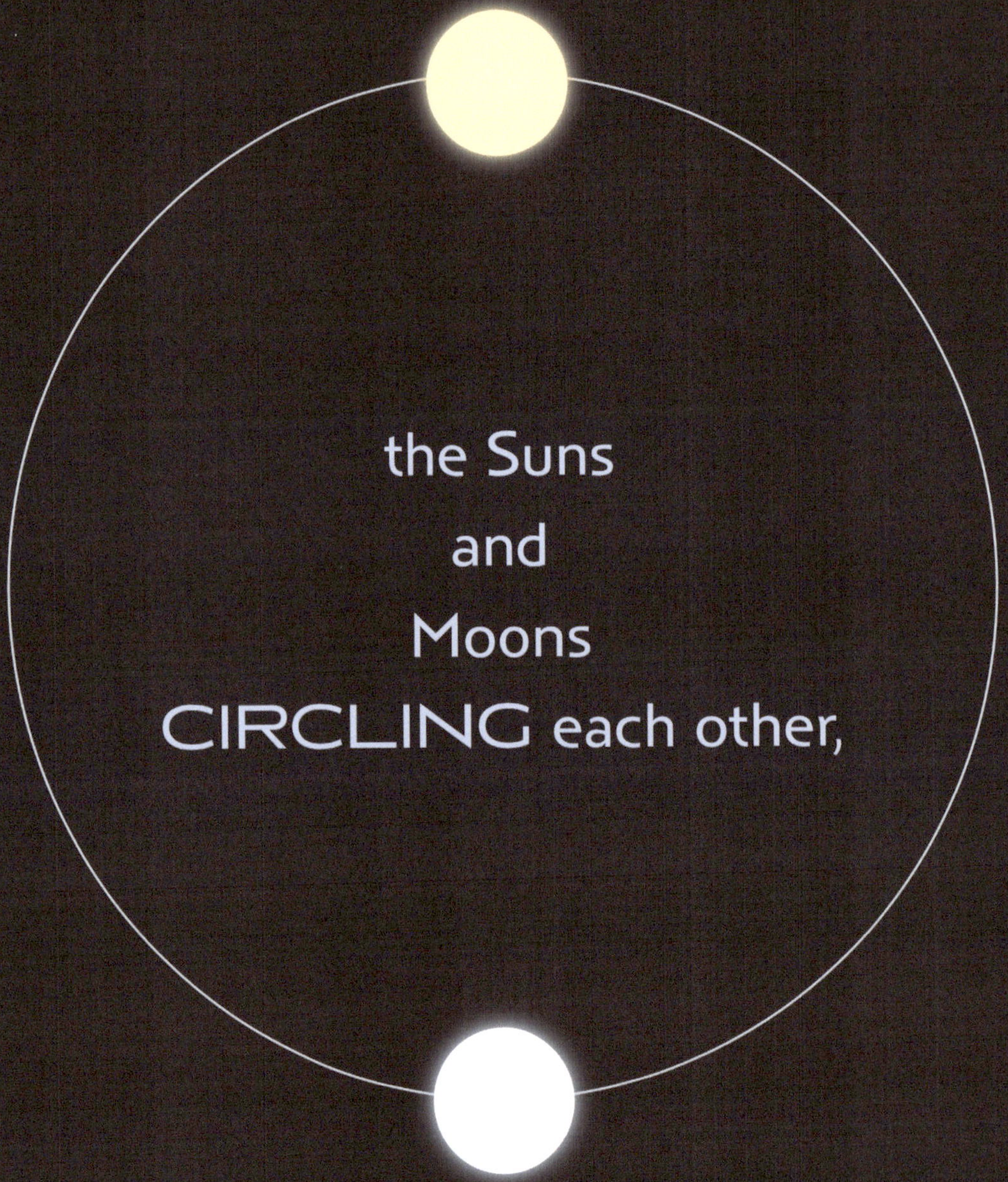

the Suns
and
Moons
CIRCLING each other,

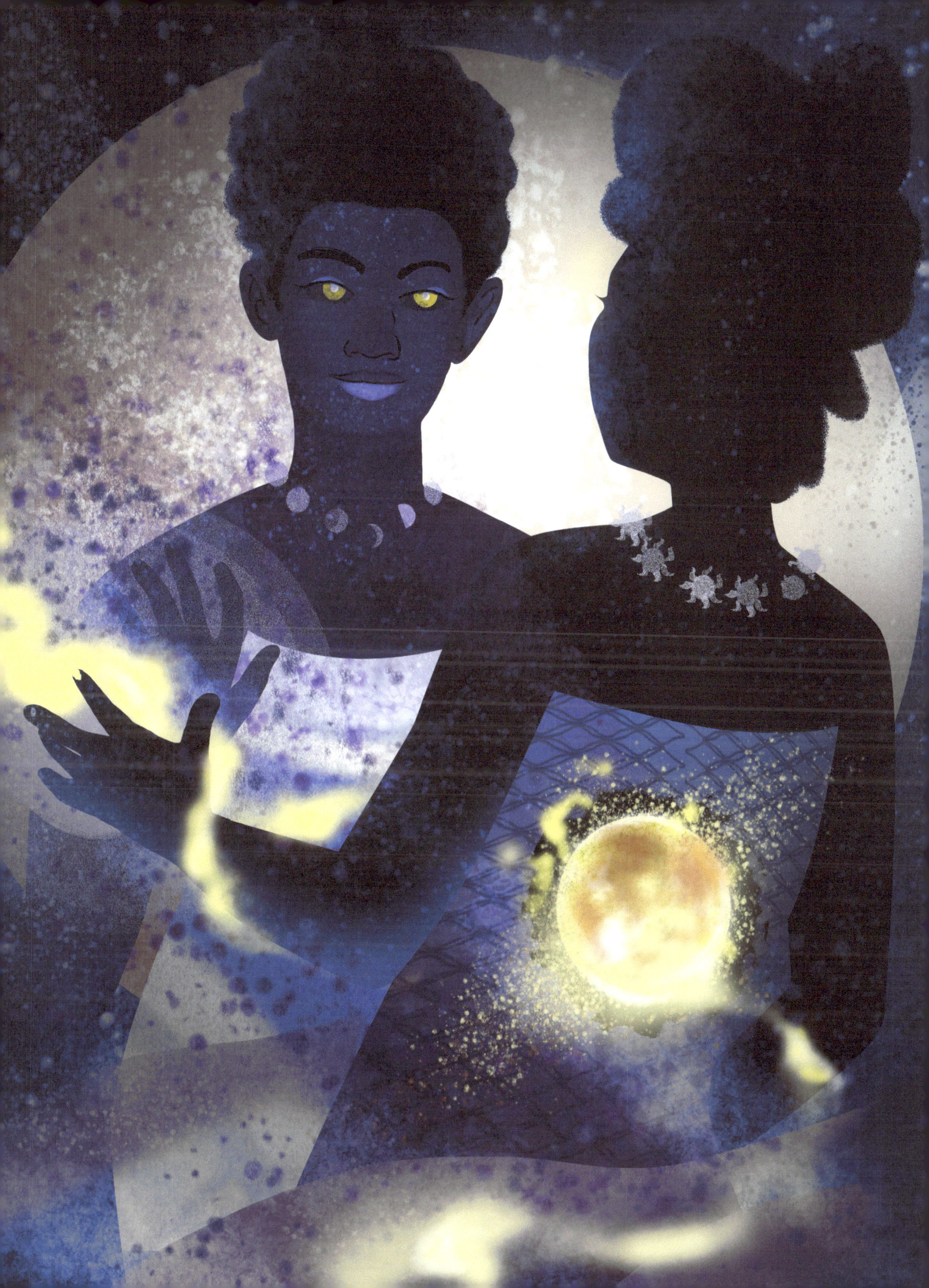

the Milky Way
WATCHING
over us,

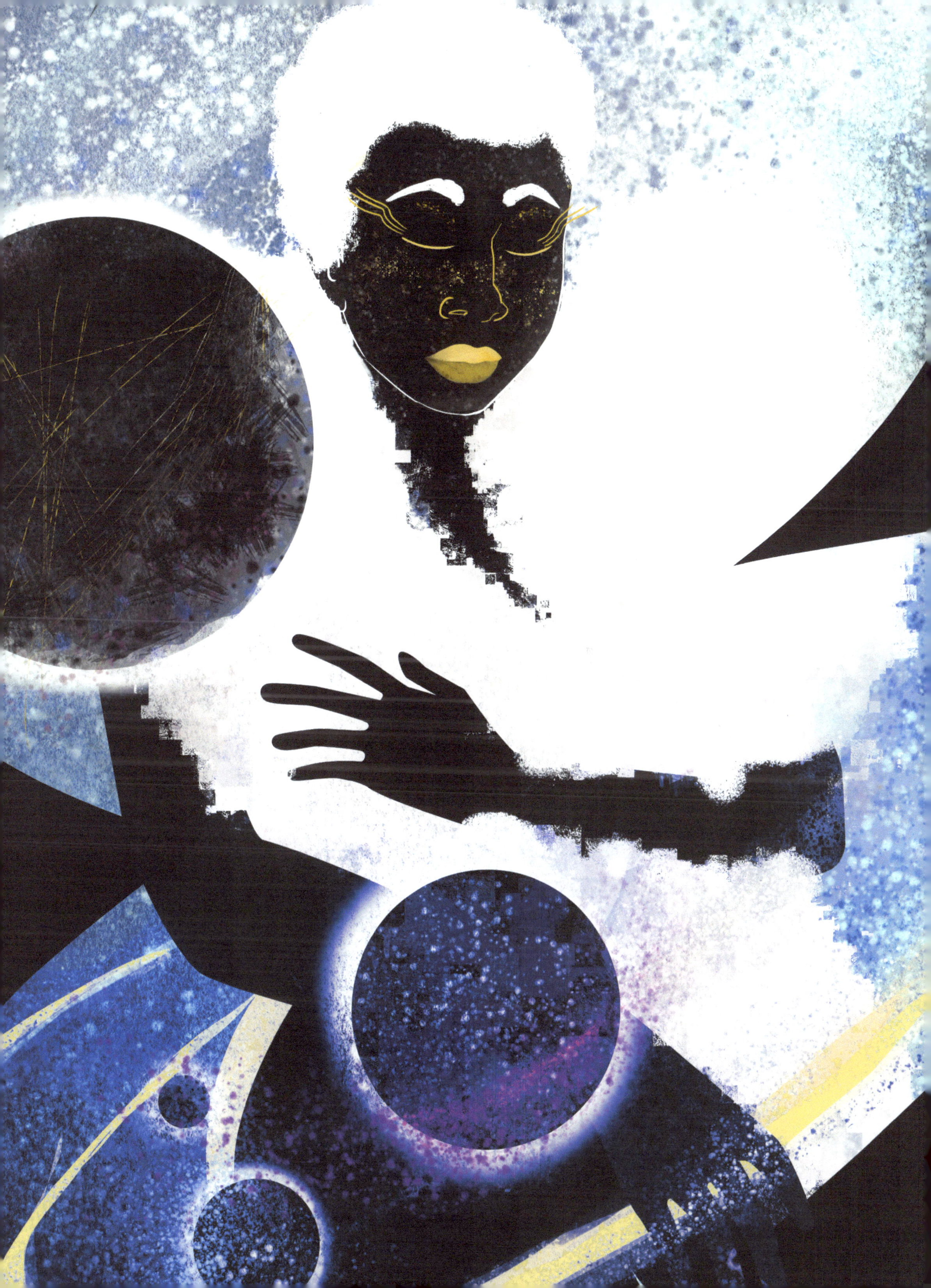

the Shooting Star
HALTING.

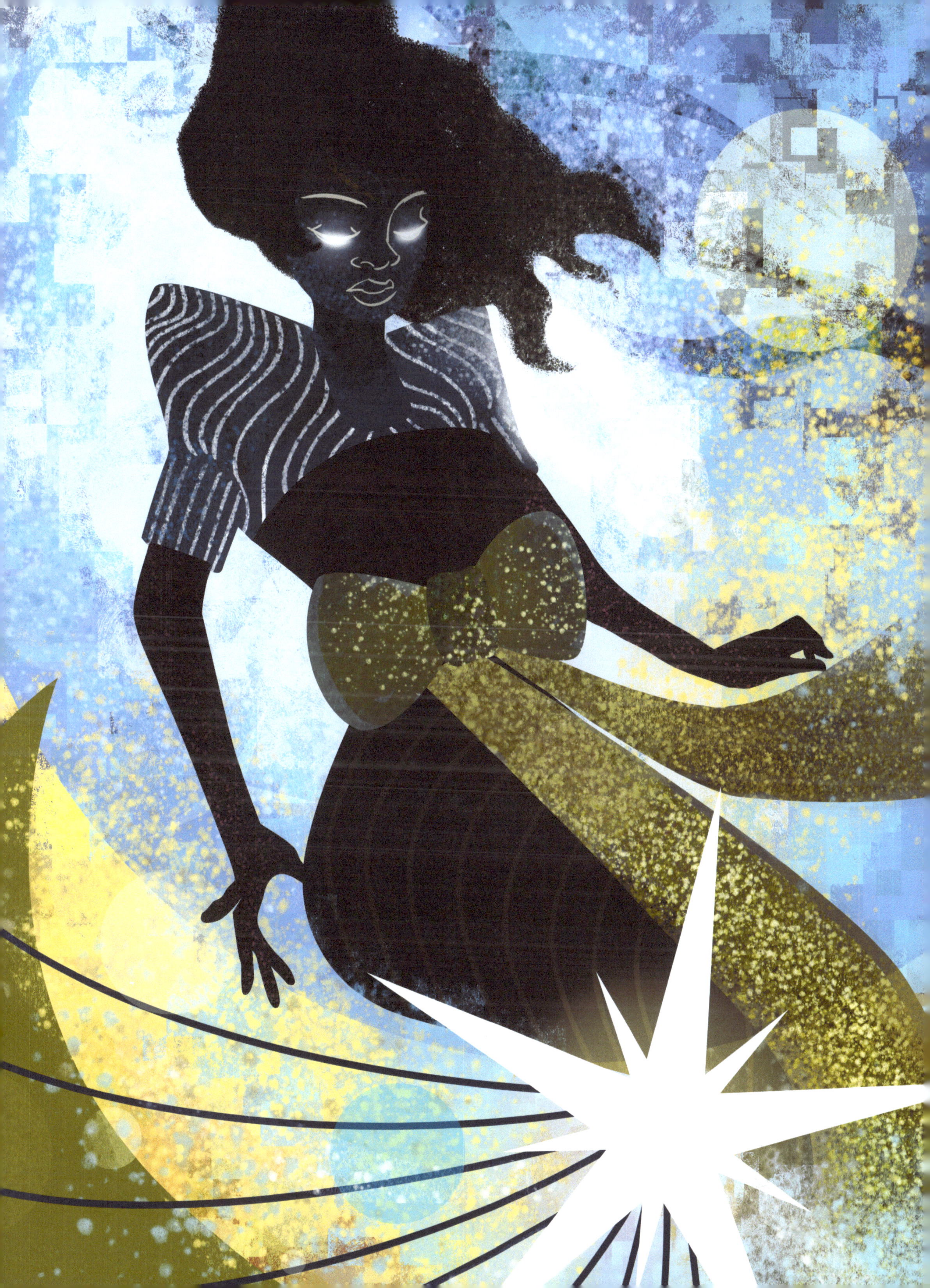

at the

EDGE

of the Universe.

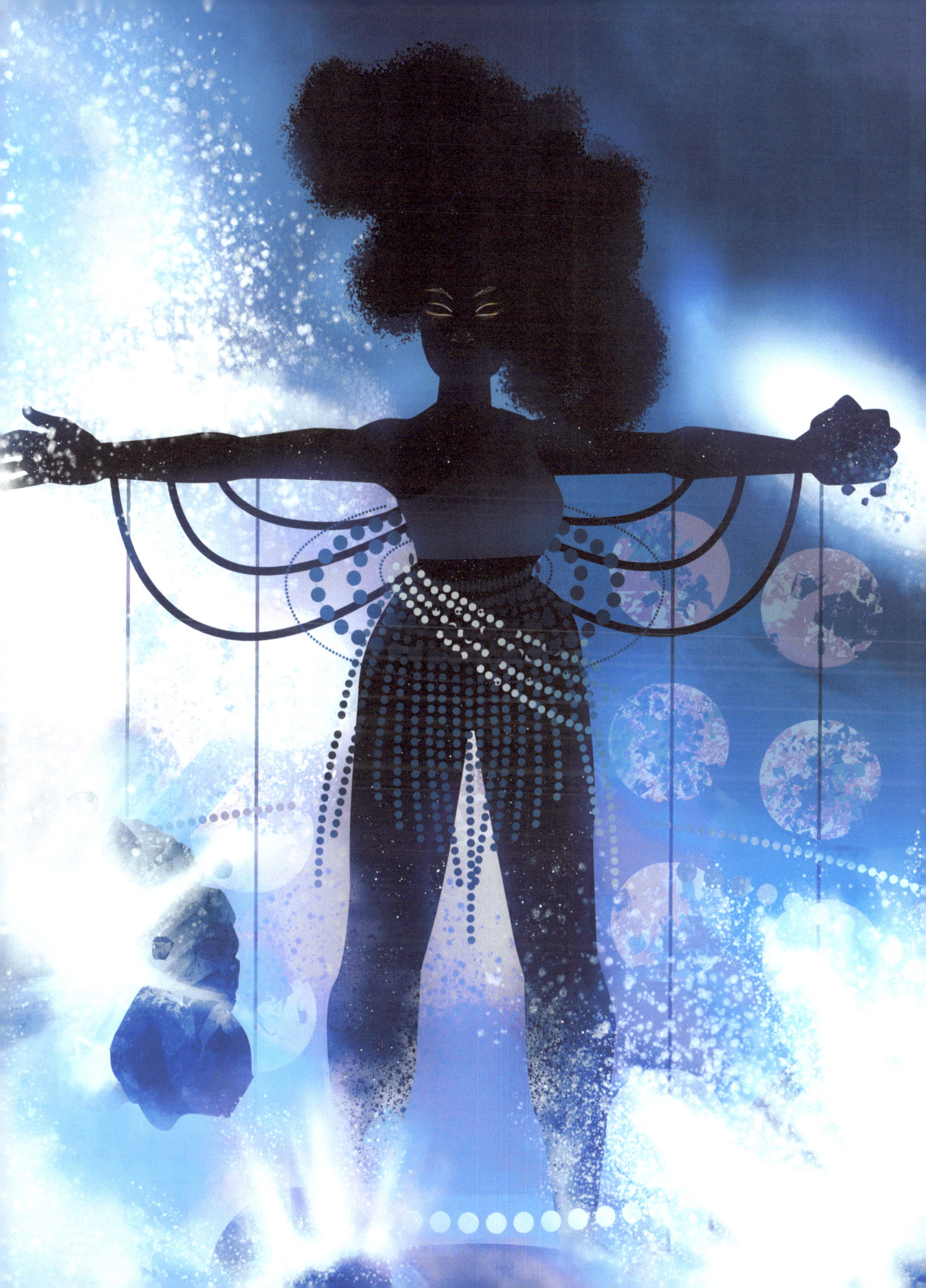

TRAVELLERS

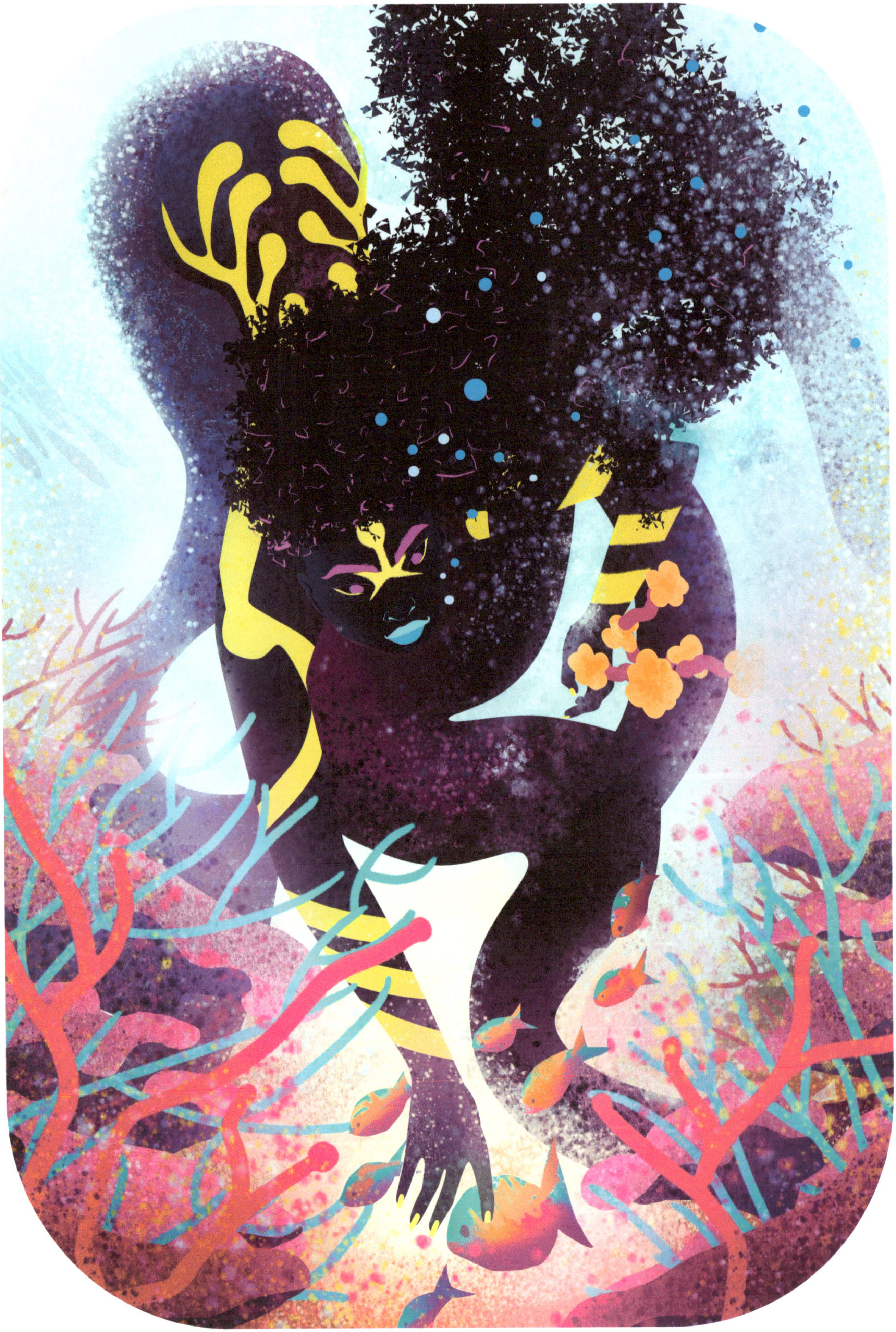

REACH

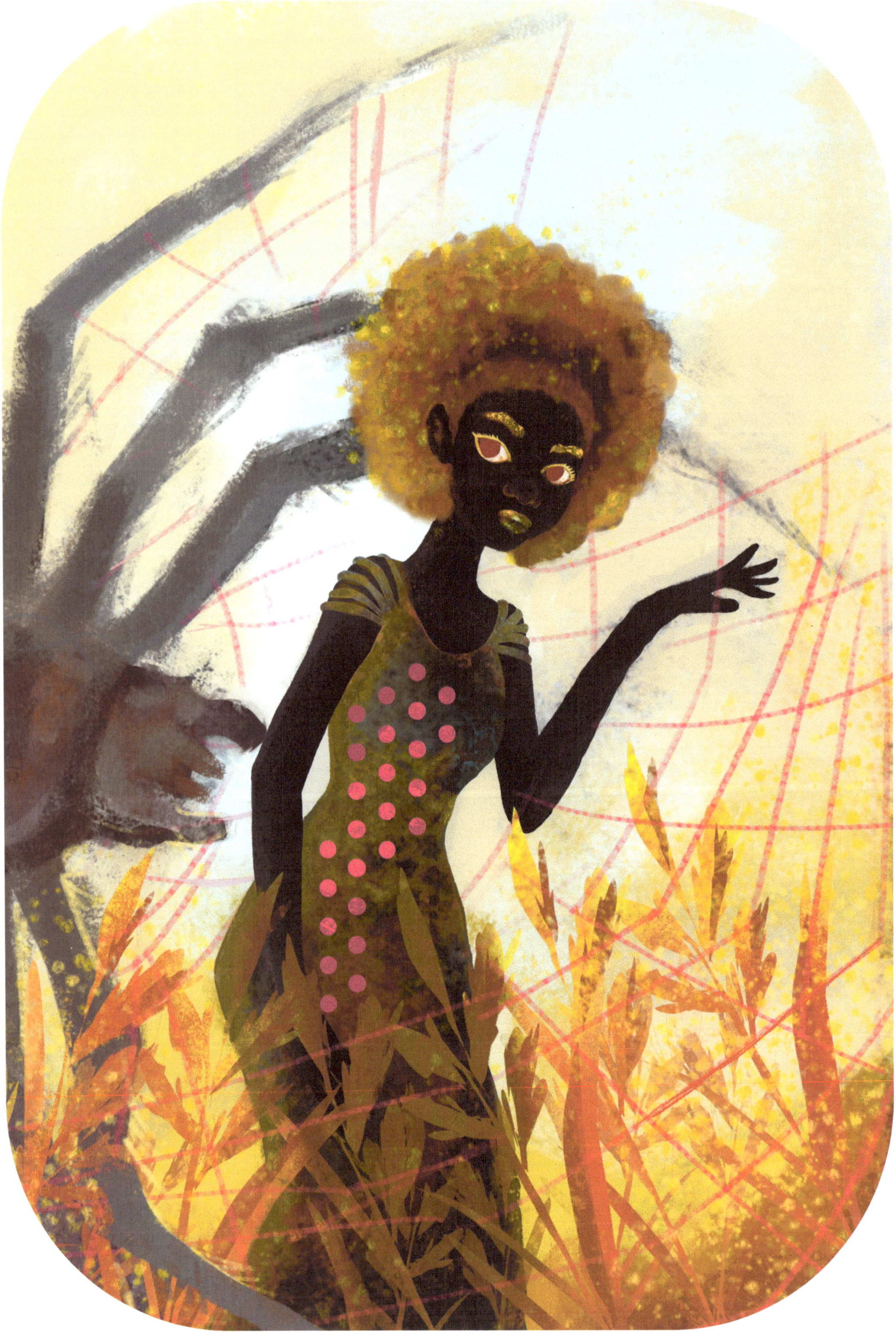

THE SPIDER

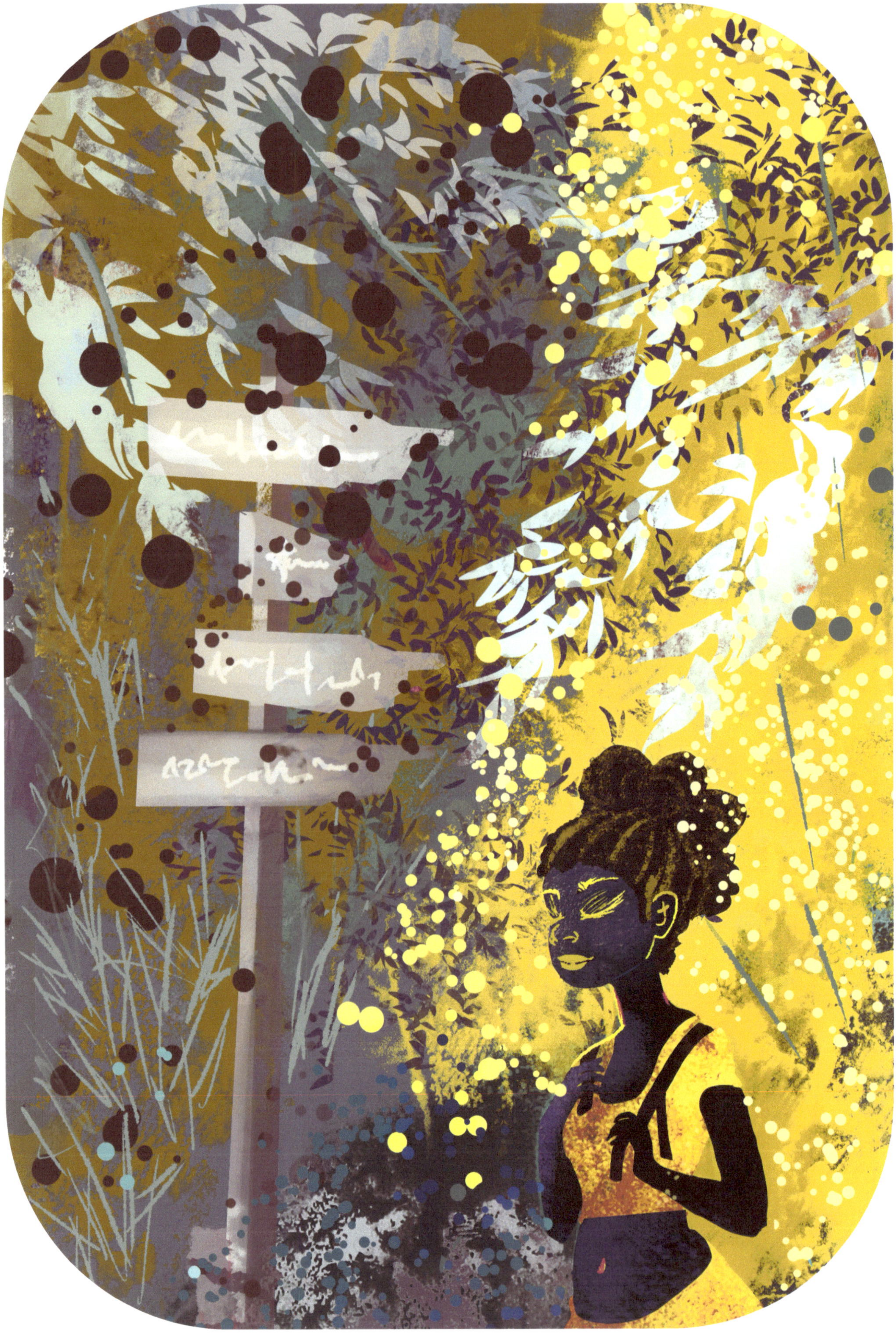

TRAVELLER

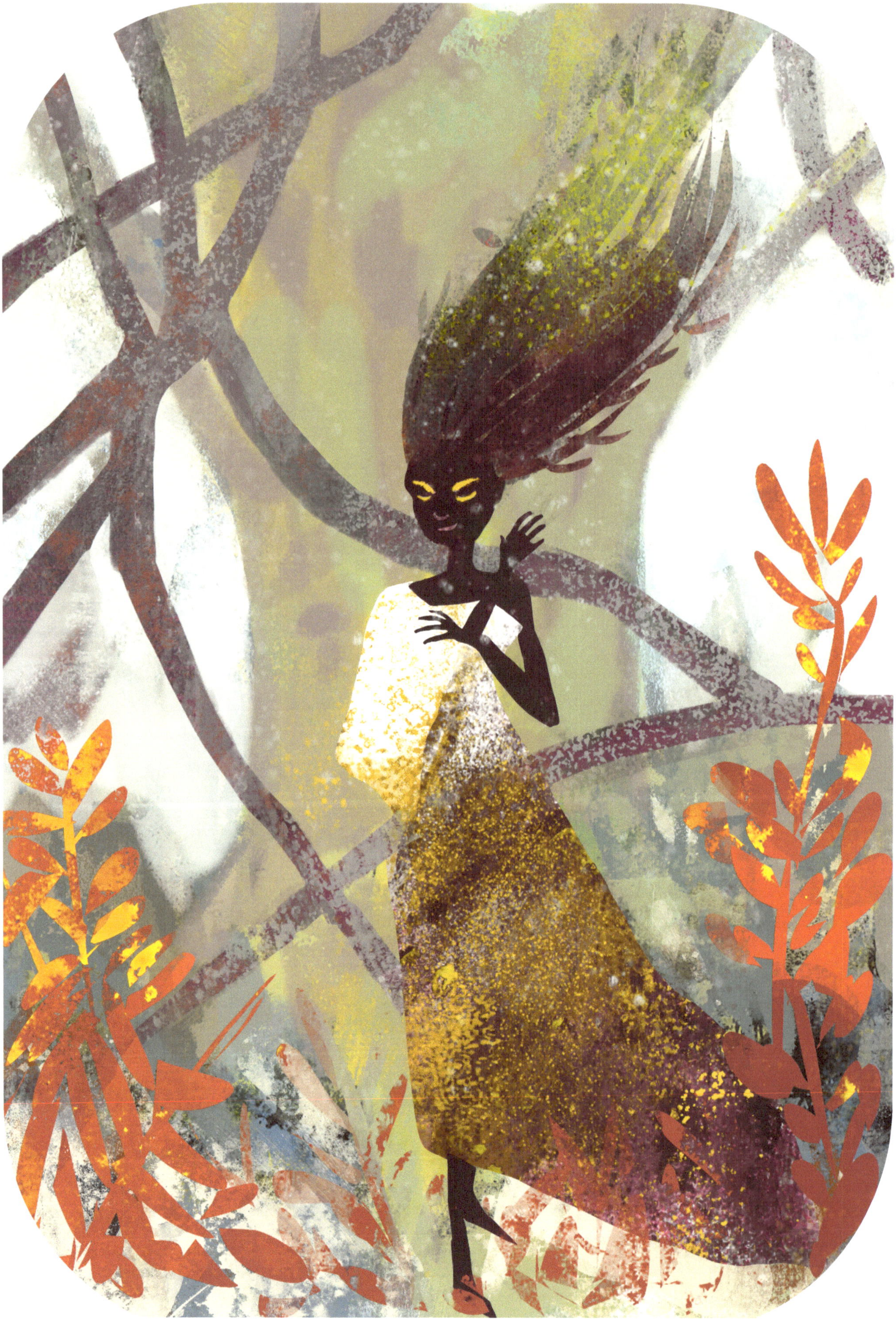

WIND SPRITE

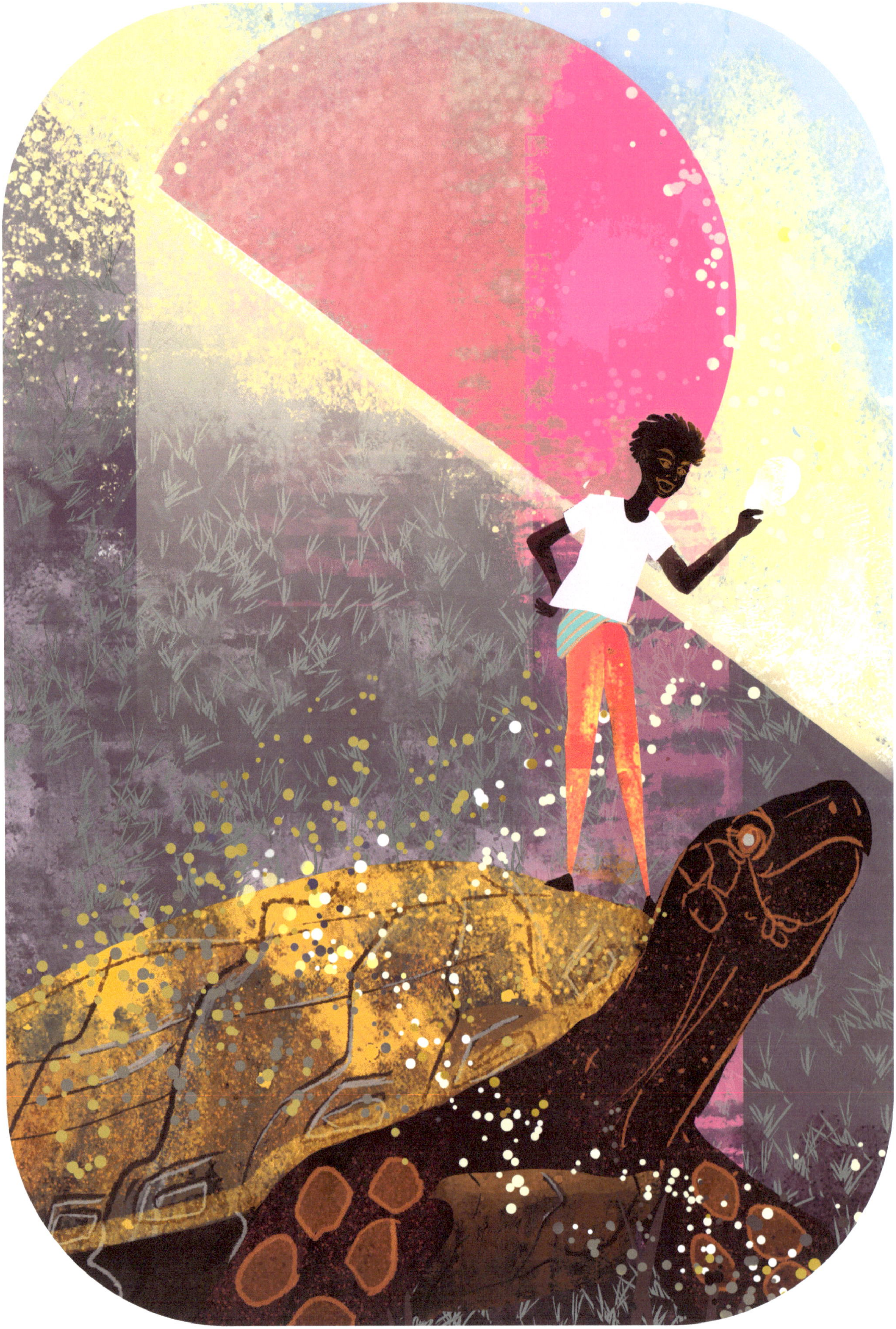

GREETINGS

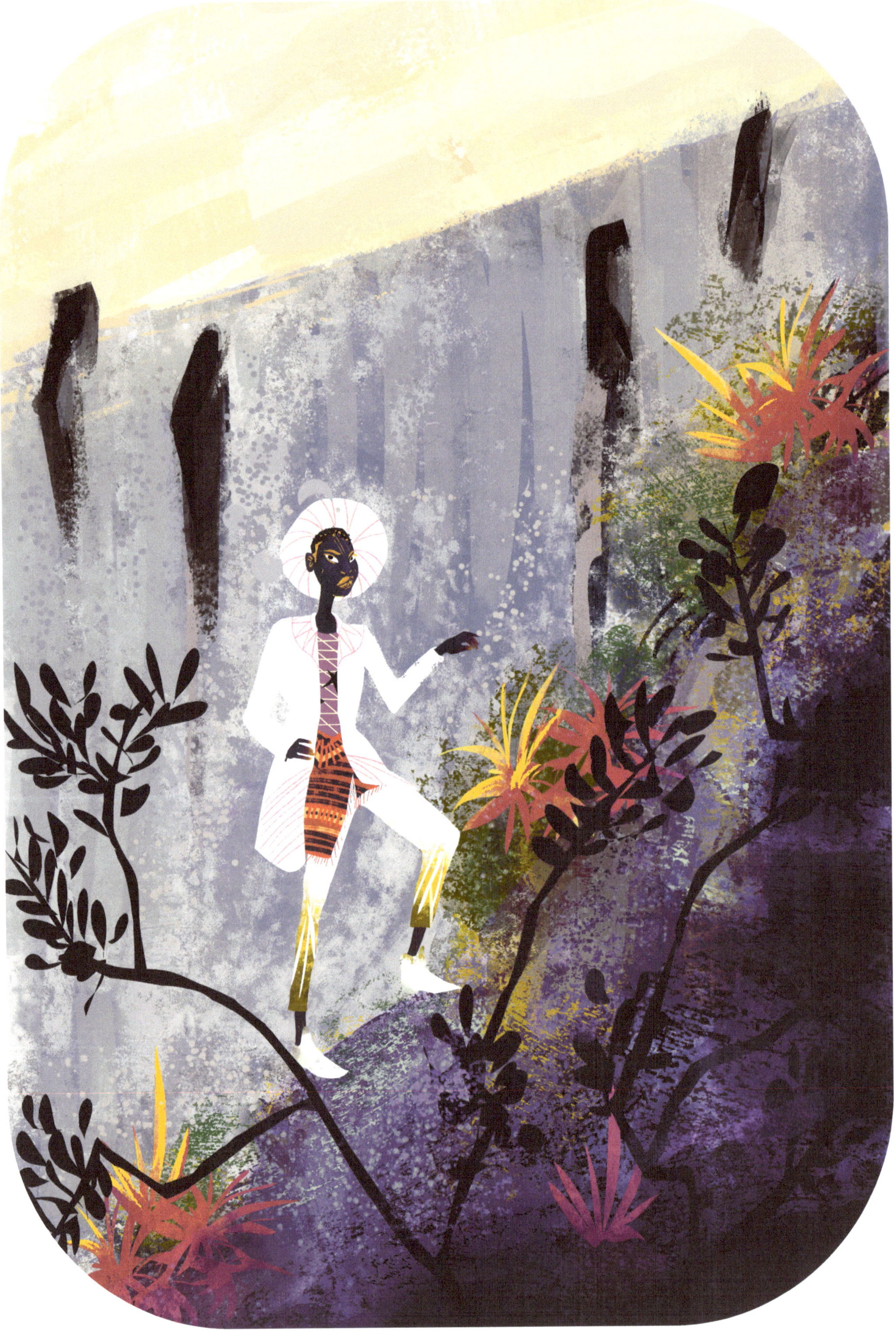

SELFIE

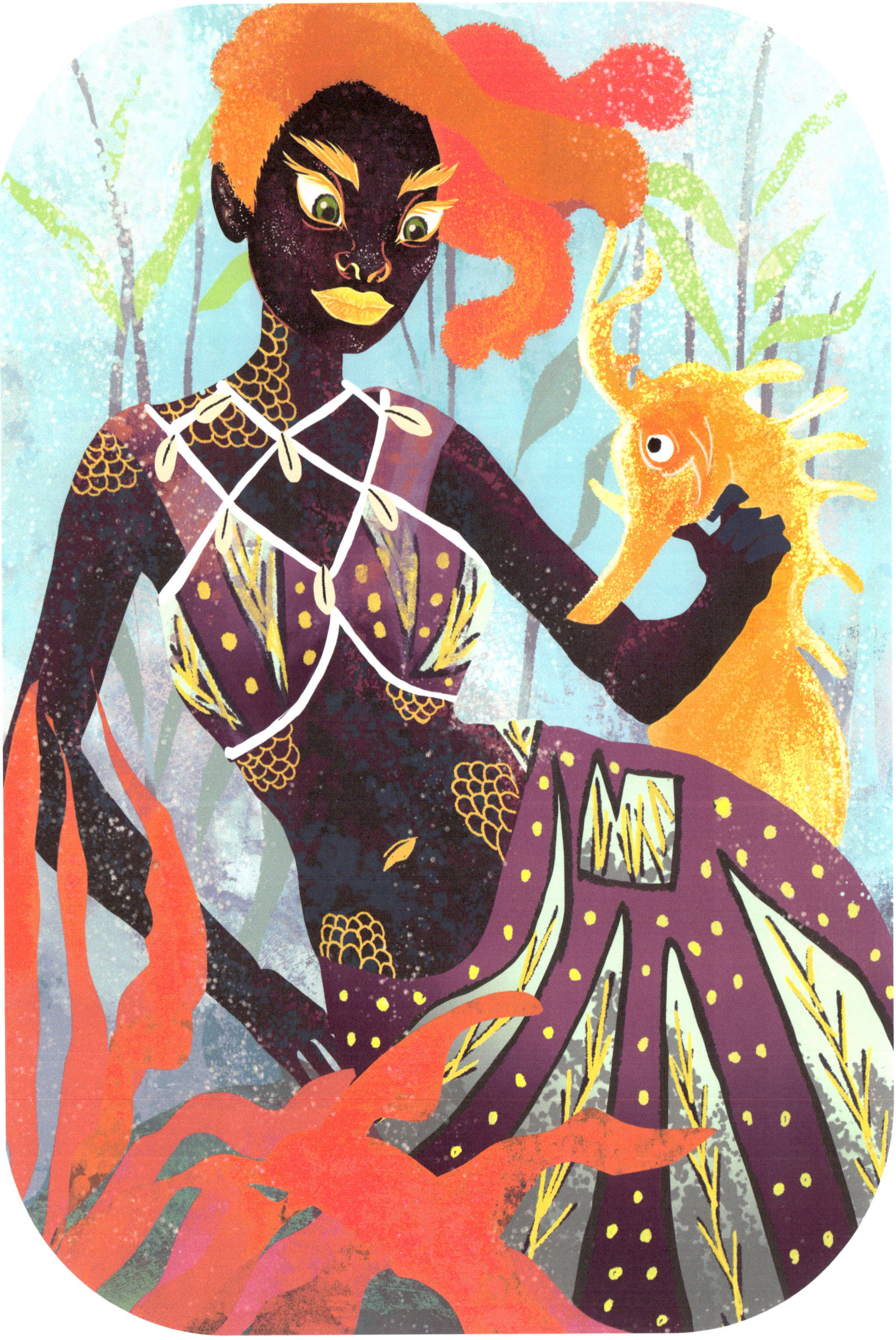

MERMAY

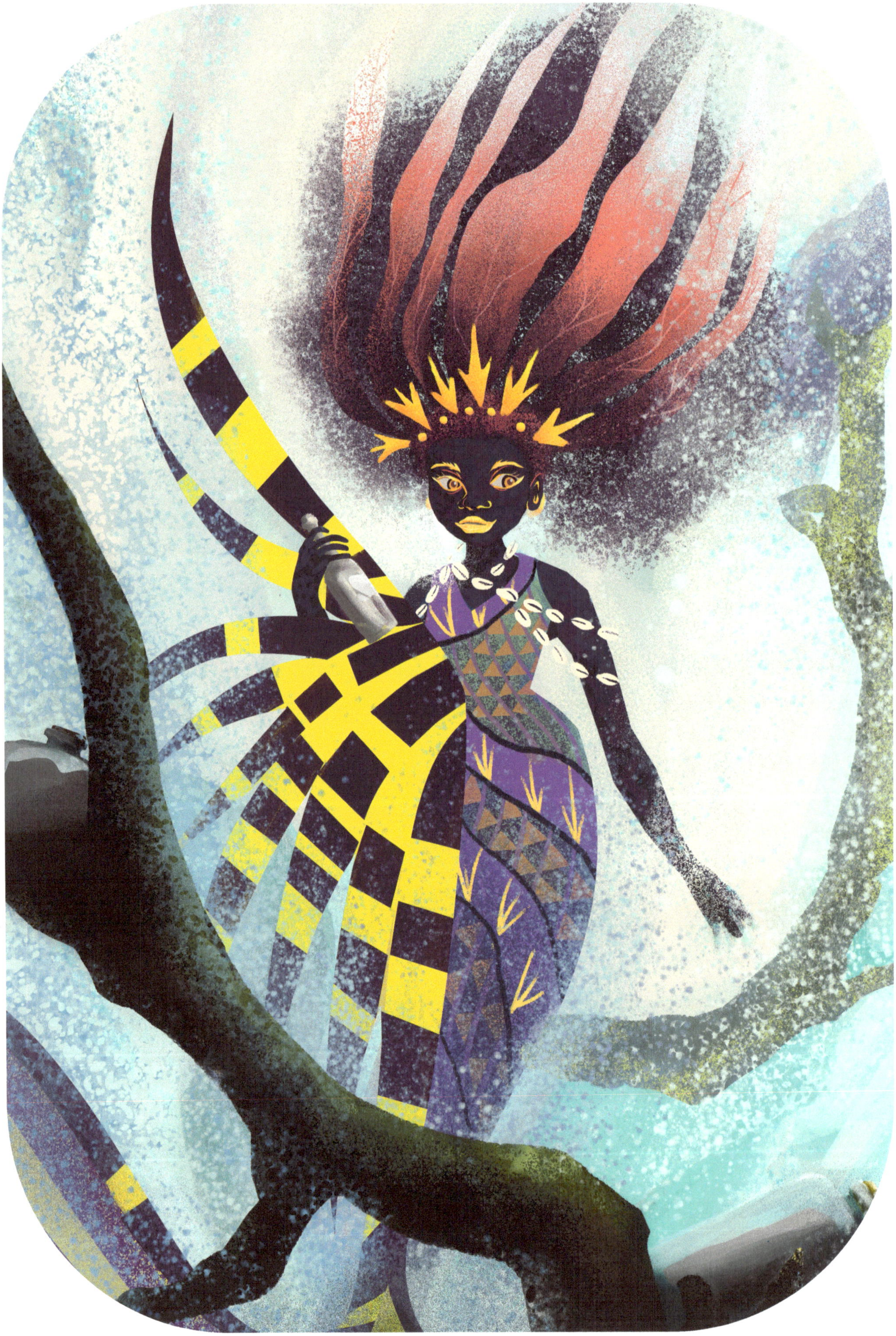

THE COLLECTOR

BRIEF CHANCE OF MOONLIGHT

A STORY ABOUT A MOON PRINCESS
WHO ESCAPES TO EARTH FOR A NIGHT

BY
AKEM

BRIEF CHANCE OF MOONLIGHT

The night brightens around me, and I drop into the mud like a scared rabbit. The cool mud makes me shiver and the tall grass scratches my delicate, dark skin. I grin at the sensations—it's a victory to be this uncomfortable.

Above me, the clouds part as a moonbeam cuts through them to touch Earth.

I'm resigned to what comes next, the traitorous moonlight giving away my position.

My Aerie drops through the moonbeam feet first, striking the ground in a puff of dust. Her knees bend slightly, and her shimmering white cape flies upwards and outward like a water spout. She straightens as the moonbeam that delivered her to Earth dims then blinks out and the clouds huddle together again.

I watch her as she stands tall and commanding among the rocks and trees. Her limbs are darker than the night—not even the shining armour she wears illuminates her skin. She scans the darkness, hands on the pommel of her sword, before she lifts her face towards the clouds to ask a question. Soon, a sliver of moonlight kisses her face, activating the glittering stardust scattered there.

I slump deeper into the grass, knowing that the moonlight's whisper has told where her wayward Princess has hidden. In the distance, her head turns sharply towards me like a compass.

Her first step is savage, her bright heel hitting the ground in warning. It groans under her weight, sinking with each of her steps.

The star that guards me. My protector. My sword.

She comes for me.

"But I've only just arrived," I mutter. I wonder which star spotted me on my way down to Earth. But the stars and the moon are now hidden by the clouds, and only a brief chance of moonlight had delivered myself and my Aerie to this location.

I hear the ground groan under her weight as she walks. She gives me time to contemplate the gravity of my stupidity with her slow approach, instead of lightening her weight and reaching me with a leap. An Aerie—a star in human form—controls their own gravity. Outside the glittering palace walls on the moon, she could rest solidly on the ground should she wish it.

A shiver runs involuntarily through my body and I wrap my arms around myself. I had made a miscalculation when I slipped her guard; my night dress is too thin for Earth's weather.

I fidget in the cold, wet grass before I decide to shamble forward to sit by the small lake in front of me. My hiding spot has been discovered. There's no need to be uncomfortable for the upcoming scolding.

I feel the smooth pebbles by the lake, listen to the waves, and ignore my doom approaching. I focus on feeling everything, and record it in my memories. I probably won't be coming back to Earth after this. So I lift my face to the light rain that begins to fall, delighting as it gently pats my face. I enjoy the oddity of water falling from the sky. Even though my bones ache like they're being crushed by Earth's gravity, I marvel. I was below the clouds, among grass, touched by rain.

On the Moon, everything is dry and cool: the palace walls, the sand outside the palace, the stones I cast up into space only to have them float gently before me. It's an odd sensation to be affected by things that didn't exist in my mind except for in stories.

I reach out to brush the soft, white spines of a ball-like flower. Its white seeds detach from the seed-head and float upward into the air. I gape at the spines' dance as they float away; the movement is magical in the diffused moonlight.

When my Aerie arrives, I don't look up. Instead, I slap a flower cloud into the air.

"Princess," she greets me.

Her armour glows with trapped moonlight, illuminating the muddy lakeshore and my dirty feet covered in scratches. I suddenly feel embarrassed as I straighten and pat my puffy hair awkwardly, brushing away some twigs and leaves that it had acquired on my adventures. My landing had not been as upright as hers—I had greeted Earth face-first in an inelegant sprawl.

Her face is a dark void so I can't see her expression, though I know it must hold annoyance. I square my shoulders and lift my chin proudly.

She unsheathes her shining sword. I recoil, blinking at its bright glow. Starlight reveals an Aerie's face, but moonlight reveals mine, so I turn away from it, hoping to hide my adventure's scratches and bruises.

After a long silence, I turn back just as she stabs the sword into the ground. The earth cracks like a mirror where the glowing blade meets it. I snatch my foot back from a spiderweb of lines that reach towards me and tuck my heels under me.

I rest my hands on my thighs and brace for the lecture.

"Are you having a good time?" she asks. She raises her finger and touches where her lips would be, a sign that she is struggling not to laugh.

My mouth gapes open. I had expected anger and irritation, not amusement.

My Aerie kneels beside me and gently asks, "What have you discovered today?"

I impulsively reach out and feel her shadowed face. The curve of her cheek shows she is smiling, pretending that she can't see that I am hurt.

I drop my hand. Relieved, I dare to pout. I slump, pulling my muddy gown from my chest with two fingers in distaste—admitting a slight (the slightest!) error in judgement when she gives me space to do so.

"The ground is hard and the bushes are vicious," I say petulantly.

"And the water is wet."

Her hand tugs the curls of my hair, its puffy fullness drooping with water.

I pull away, pretending offence—but grin in relief.

Shock rising on her face was the last I'd seen of her on the Moon.

•••

The Travelling Room on the Moon was quiet and unguarded when I'd happened upon it during Sleep Time. Silently, my Aerie trailed behind me—she'd given up on coaxing me into bed.

In the Travelling Room, the Travelling Sphere hovered over the waist-high pillar in the centre of the circular dome. The yellow glow from the sphere was dim as if it had settled down for the night.

It was rare to see the Room unguarded, but no one would dare enter the Queen's personal Travelling Room. I had travelled through the Sphere before, always to some boring formal occasion and always with my mother gripping my hand tightly. But I'd never been to the place I truly wanted to go, a place that was so close to home.

The Earth gleamed like a pristine jewel from the Moon, so vivid against the black of space. Before I knew it, I found myself darting into the room, bare feet slapping hard against cool marble. My eyes fixed on that vision, I slammed my palm on the Travelling Sphere so hard that it bumped into the pillar below it.

"Princess! Stop!" I heard the cry from my Aerie as the Travelling Sphere lit up to fill the room with its moonglow. Then the moonbeam's light carried me through space in an intoxicating, breathless ride.

•••

My Aerie is definitely amused. Thankful, I grab the edge of her shimmering cape and wrap it around my cold body.

"Princess..." She sighs. But she lets me wriggle under her muscular arm. Her armour is cool at first, but I soon feel the metal increase its warmth and my shivers abate.

I absently rub the scrape along my elbow and try to squeeze the water from my nightgown. Beneath me, mud squelches through my toes. She waits until I get comfortable, tightening her arm around my shoulders as I shift my feet back and forth in the muck, trying to decide if I enjoy the sensation of the sticky mess between my cold toes.

"Have you been down here before?" I ask, though I know the answer.

She looks up at the sky, searching for a way out, but the clouds block our path back home.

I relax. She can't call the moonbeam now.

"Once. When the Queen was young, she wanted to see a real rabbit. She heard the people of the Earth thought there was a rabbit on the moon."

I smile innocently—I know this story by heart.

"And did you catch one?" I tease.

"In time, but first we had to find out what a rabbit was by speaking to the local people." She pauses. "It didn't go well. We spent a full day trapped on Earth when the sun rose. Some of the locals thought we were gods, and some thought we were demons."

I am surprised. This is a part of the story I haven't heard before. I wait for her to finish, but she speaks no more. I feel tension roll through her. She pulls her sword from the ground and continues to diligently search for a thread of moonlight.

I didn't want this adventure to be over, but I now understood her urgency. We need to leave before the rising sun—my mother, it seemed, had left out certain details of her first journey.

Once back on the Moon, the Queen might ground me for decades.

"Let's find a rabbit then and bring it back home!" I say, as if the idea has just come to me. "We can complete the tale and there'll be a rabbit on the moon."

She looks down and I can almost feel her eyes narrow.

I try to skip away but all I manage is an upward bounce before her grip on my shoulders holds me back. I settle down, but keep my eyes fixed on the illuminated ground around me as I search for a soft, round creature with long ears and feet like I'd seen embroidered into my mother's tapestry robe. The Queen often wore this robe often at night as she roamed around her chambers, and when she came to bid me goodnight. Before she left my bedside, I would ask about the faded rabbit that bounced through the grass and trees on the robe.

My Aerie sighs: she's seen through my plan. She frees her sword from the ground and ignites the moonlight trapped in the sword shaft.

I turn my face away from the glow to hide my disappointment.

A large sphere of light brightens our immediate surroundings. Earth looks magical: the blade illuminates shadows under the grass and bushes, and startled raindrops glimmering on shrubs.

My Aerie steps back from me and points the sword at my bare feet. Light uncurls from the sword and wraps my feet in its glow. When the sword's brightness fades, my feet are shod in moonlight.

I smile, bouncing with happiness.

She shakes her head and makes a shooing motion.

I lumber into the grass before she changes her mind. My body is hunched over with gravity as I happily startle frogs and butterflies, and a bird with long legs that flaps its wings at me but doesn't fly off, standing its ground with an indignant, open beak.

Behind me, my Aerie tracks my every movement. As time goes on, the world subtly leans towards the still Aerie. The lake water creeps to her toes, the treetops bow towards her. Even I am caught in her gravity, circling her on an invisible tether.

I think she indulges me because the moonlight doesn't break the clouds, and she doesn't think I'll actually find anything.

Sooner than I imagined, the day brightens. Then—out of the corner of my eye, I see long ear tips, quivering in the grass. I stumble forward with a cry; my tired body feels heavier than when I am in my formal robes, weighed down with metals from every world in our solar system.

In that moment, a moonbeam breaks through the clouds, catching the wide-eyed rabbit in its shine as it bounces away from me.

I leap into the moonbeam. How stupid—a moment later, I feel my Aerie's grip around my waist. I wriggle urgently and stretch, catching the startled rabbit and hugging it to my chest.

Then my Aerie and I separate into millions of tiny lights and shoot back up to the moon.

When we arrive, the Queen waits in her night robe, pacing back and forth in front of the Travelling Room. Her hair is wild and unbound by ceremonial wraps and combs. She rushes toward me, scolding me before I'm set on the cool marble floor by my Aerie. I stand at attention in her shining palace, muddy footprints dirtying the floor, while the Queen lectures me on the dangers of predatory animals, of killing weather, of humans and their weapons. Her dark face sparkles with moon dust, twinkling with anger.

She ignores the ball of fur I clutch against my chest until the rabbit moves, long ears perking up as its face pokes out over my arm to peer at her. She pauses her tirade, eyes widening, then reaches out a long finger to tentatively rub the rabbit's soft head.

I keep my eyes fixed on her robes and trace the faded woven scene on her floor-length robes: an Aerie and her Queen, chasing after a rabbit between tall trees on Earth in the moonlight.

I smile secretly.

Behind me is the Earth, shining like a gleaming jewel; to my side is my Aerie; and in my arms, finally, is the rabbit on the moon.

AKEM IS A WRITER AND ARTIST THAT WORKS IN THE ANIMATION AND PUBLISHING INDUSTRY. SHE CREATES TO SEE WHAT'S INSIDE HER HEAD.

MYTHIC TEXTURE IS A COMPILATION OF ART WORK FROM A FIVE YEAR PERIOD. HER SHORT STORIES CAN BE FOUND IN CANADIAN MAGAZINES LIKE **AUGUR MAGAZINE**, **POLAR BOREALIS**, **PULP LITERATURE**, AND THE **CAPILANO REVIEW**.

SHE HAS WORKED AS AN ARTIST ON **SPIDERVERSE 2**, **YOUNG LOVE**, **CARMEN SANDIEGO**, AND OTHER ANIMATED SHOWS IN VANCOUVER,BC.

OTHER WORKS

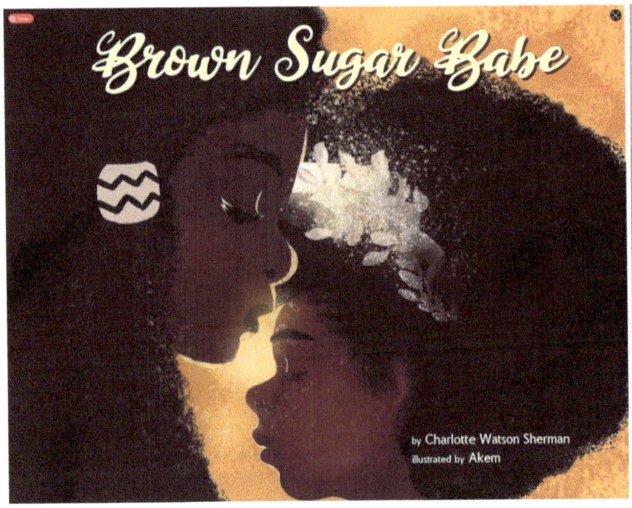

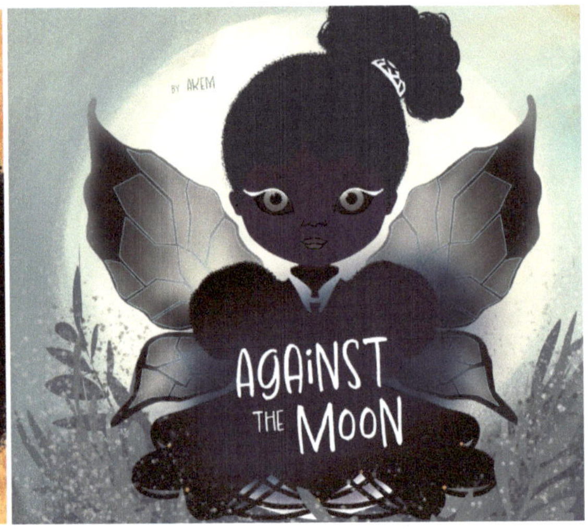

SIGN UP TO THE MAILING LIST ON **WWW.MYTHICTEXTURE.COM** TO HEAR OF UPCOMING RELEASES AND PROMOTIONS FOR **MYTHIC TEXTURE MEDIA**, A PUBLISHER OF WORKS BY AKEM.

www.ingramcontent.com/pod-product-compliance
Ingram Content Group UK Ltd.
Pitfield, Milton Keynes, MK11 3LW, UK
UKHW061028310726
14090UKWH00026B/295
* 9 7 8 1 7 3 8 8 4 0 6 3 2 *